The Living Library

Rubáiyát

OF OMAR KHAYYÁM

RENDERED INTO ENGLISH VERSE BY

Edward FitzGerald

ILLUSTRATED BY JOSEPH LOW

The World Publishing Company

CLEVELAND AND NEW YORK

The Living Library

IS PUBLISHED BY *The World Publishing Company*

2231 West 110th Street · Cleveland 2 · Ohio

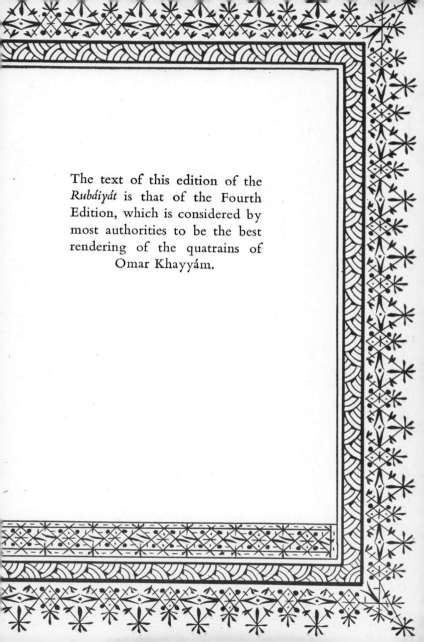

The text of this edition of the *Rubáiyát* is that of the Fourth Edition, which is considered by most authorities to be the best rendering of the quatrains of Omar Khayyám.

OMAR KHAYYÁM

The Astronomer-Poet of Persia

OMAR KHAYYÁM was born at Naishápúr
in Khorassán in the latter half of our
Eleventh, and died within the First
Quarter of our Twelfth Century. The
slender Story of his Life is curiously
twined about that of two other very
considerable Figures in their Time and
Country: one of whom tells the Story of
all Three. This was Nizám-ul-Mulk,
Vizier to Alp Arslán the Son, and Malik
Shah the Grandson, of Toghrul Beg
the Tartar, who had wrested Persia from
the feeble Successor of Mahmúd the

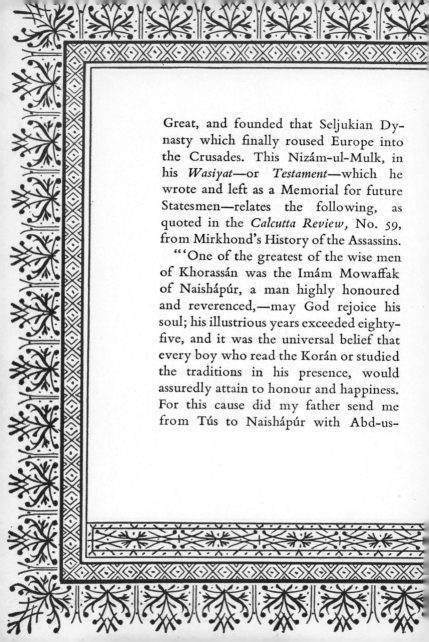

Great, and founded that Seljukian Dynasty which finally roused Europe into the Crusades. This Nizám-ul-Mulk, in his *Wasiyat*—or *Testament*—which he wrote and left as a Memorial for future Statesmen—relates the following, as quoted in the *Calcutta Review*, No. 59, from Mirkhond's History of the Assassins.

"'One of the greatest of the wise men of Khorassán was the Imám Mowaffak of Naishápúr, a man highly honoured and reverenced,—may God rejoice his soul; his illustrious years exceeded eighty-five, and it was the universal belief that every boy who read the Korán or studied the traditions in his presence, would assuredly attain to honour and happiness. For this cause did my father send me from Tús to Naishápúr with Abd-ussamad, the doctor of law, that I might employ myself in study and learning under the guidance of that illustrious teacher. Towards me he ever turned an eye of favour and kindness, and as his pupil I felt for him extreme affection and devotion, so that I passed four years in his service. When I first came there, I found two other pupils of mine own age newly arrived, Hakim Omar Khayyám, and the ill-fated Ben Sabbáh. Both were endowed with sharpness of wit and the highest natural powers; and we three formed a close friendship together. When the Imám rose from his lectures, they used to join me, and we repeated to each other the lessons we had heard. Now Omar was a native of Naishápúr, while Hasan Ben Sabbáh's father was one Ali, a man of austere life and practice, but heretical in his creed and doctrine. One day Hasan said to me and to Khayyám, "It is a universal belief that the pupils of the Imám Mowaffak will attain to fortune. Now, even if we *all* do not attain thereto, without doubt one of us will; what then shall be our mutual pledge and bond?" We answered, "Be it what you please." "Well," he said, "let us make a vow, that to whomsoever this fortune falls, he shall share it equally with the rest, and reserve no pre-eminence for himself." "Be it so," we both replied, and on those terms we mutually pledged our words. Years rolled on, and I went from Khorassán to Transoxiana, and wandered to Ghazni and Cabul; and when I returned, I was invested with office, and rose to be administrator of affairs during the Sultanate of Sultan Alp Arslán.'

"He goes on to state, that years passed by, and both his old school-friends found him out, and came and claimed a share in his good fortune, according to the school-day vow. The Vizier was generous and kept his word. Hasan demanded a place in the government, which the Sultan granted at the Vizier's request; but discontented with a gradual rise, he plunged into the maze of intrigue of an oriental court, and, failing in a base attempt to supplant his benefactor, he was disgraced and fell. After many mishaps and wanderings, Hasan became the head of the Persian sect of the *Ismailians,* —a party of fanatics who had long murmured in obscurity, but rose to an evil eminence under the guidance of his strong and evil will. In A.D. 1090, he seized the castle of Alamút, in the province of Rúdbar, which lies in the mountainous tract south of the Caspian Sea; and it was from this mountain home he obtained that evil celebrity among the Crusaders as the OLD MAN OF THE MOUNTAINS, and spread terror through the Mohammedan world; and it is yet disputed whether the word *Assassin,* which they have left in the language of modern Europe as their dark memorial, is derived from the *hashish*, or opiate of hemp-leaves (the Indian *bhang*), with which they maddened themselves to the sullen pitch of oriental desperation, or from the name of the founder of the dynasty, whom we have seen in his quiet collegiate days, at Naishápúr. One of the countless victims of the Assassin's dagger was Nizám-ul-Mulk himself, the old school-boy friend.*

"Omar Khayyám also came to the Vizier to claim his share; but not to ask for title or office. 'The greatest boon you can confer on me,' he said, 'is to

---

* Some of Omar's Rubáiyát warn us of the danger of Greatness, the instability of Fortune, and while advocating Charity to all Men, recommending us to be too intimate with none. Attár makes Nizám-ul-Mulk use the very words of his friend Omar [Rub. xxviii.], "When Nizám-ul-Mulk was in the Agony (of death) he said, 'Oh God! I am passing away in the hand of the wind.'" [Note: in this Fourth Edition, the words of Omar are rendered into English as follows—"I came like Water, and like Wind I go."—The Publishers.]

let me live in a corner under the shadow of your fortune, to spread wide the advantages of Science, and pray for your long life and prosperity.' The Vizier tells us, that, when he found Omar was really sincere in his refusal, he pressed him no further, but granted him a yearly pension of 1200 *mithkáls* of gold, from the treasury of Naishápúr.

"At Naishápúr thus lived and died Omar Khayyám, 'busied,' adds the Vizier, 'in winning knowledge of every kind, and especially in Astronomy, wherein he attained to a very high pre-eminence. Under the Sultanate of Malik Shah, he came to Merv, and obtained great praise for his proficiency in science, and the Sultan showered favours upon him.'

"When Malik Shah determined to re-
form the calendar, Omar was one of the
eight learned men employed to do it,
the result was the *Jaláli* era (so called
from *Jalal-u-din*, one of the king's names)
—'a computation of time,' says Gibbon,
'which surpasses the Julian and approaches
the accuracy of the Gregorian style.' He
is also the author of some astronomical
tables, entitled 'Zíji-Maliksháhí,' and
the French have lately republished and
translated an Arabic Treatise of his on
Algebra.

"His Takhallus or poetical name
(Khayyám) signifies a Tent-maker, and
he is said to have at one time exercised
that trade, perhaps before Nizám-ul-
Mulk's generosity raised him to inde-
pendence. Many Persian poets similarly

derive their names from their occupa-
tions; thus we have Attár, 'a druggist,'
Assár, 'an oil presser,' etc.* Omar himself alludes to his name in the following
whimsical lines:—

'Khayyám, who stitched the tents of science,
  Has fallen in grief's furnace and been sud-
    denly burned;
The shears of Fate have cut the tent ropes
  of his life,
And the broker of Hope has sold him for
  nothing!'

"We have only one more anecdote to
give of his Life, and that relates to the
close; it is told in the anonymous pref-
ace which is sometimes prefixed to his

* Though all these, like our Smiths, Archers,
Millers, Fletchers, etc., may simply retain the
Surname of an hereditary calling.

poems; it has been printed in the Persian in the Appendix to Hyde's *Veterum Persarum Religio,* p. 499; and D'Herbelot alludes to it in his Bibliothéque, under *Khiam*:*—

"'It is written in the chronicles of the ancients that this King of the Wise, Omar Khayyám, died at Naishápúr in the year of the Hegira, 517 (A.D. 1123); in science he was unrivalled,—the very paragon of his age. Khwájah Nizámi of Samarcand, who was one of his pupils, relates the following story: "I often used to hold conversations with my teacher,

* "Philosophe Musulman qui a vêcu en Odeur de Sainteté dans sa Religion, vers la Fin du premier et le Commencement du second Siècle," no part of which, except the "Philosophe," can apply to *our* Khayyám.

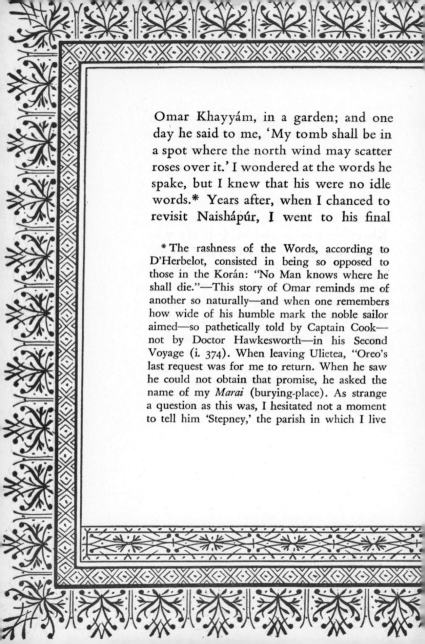

Omar Khayyám, in a garden; and one day he said to me, 'My tomb shall be in a spot where the north wind may scatter roses over it.' I wondered at the words he spake, but I knew that his were no idle words.* Years after, when I chanced to revisit Naishápúr, I went to his final

* The rashness of the Words, according to D'Herbelot, consisted in being so opposed to those in the Korán: "No Man knows where he shall die."—This story of Omar reminds me of another so naturally—and when one remembers how wide of his humble mark the noble sailor aimed—so pathetically told by Captain Cook— not by Doctor Hawkesworth—in his Second Voyage (i. 374). When leaving Ulietea, "Oreo's last request was for me to return. When he saw he could not obtain that promise, he asked the name of my *Marai* (burying-place). As strange a question as this was, I hesitated not a moment to tell him 'Stepney,' the parish in which I live

resting place, and lo! it was just outside a garden, and trees laden with fruit stretched their boughs over the garden wall, and dropped their flowers upon his tomb, so that the stone was hidden under them." ' "

Thus far—without fear of Trespass—from the *Calcutta Review*. The writer of it, on reading in India this story of Omar's Grave was reminded, he says, of Cicero's Account of finding Archimedes'

---

when in London. I was made to repeat it several times over till they could pronounce it; and then 'Stepney Marai no Toote' was echoed through an hundred mouths at once. I afterwards found the same question had been put to Mr. Forster by a man on shore; but he gave a different, and indeed more proper answer, by saying, 'No man who used the sea could say where he should be buried.' "

Tomb at Syracuse, buried in grass and weeds. I think Thorwaldsen desired to have roses grow over him; a wish religiously fulfilled for him to the present day, I believe. However, to return to Omar.

Though the Sultan "shower'd Favours upon him," Omar's Epicurean Audacity of Thought and Speech caused him to be regarded askance in his own Time and Country. He is said to have been especially hated and dreaded by the Súfis, whose Practice he ridiculed, and whose Faith amounts to little more than his own, when stript of the Mysticism and formal recognition of Islamism under which Omar would not hide. Their Poets, including Háfiz, who are (with the exception of Firdausi) the most considerable in Persia, borrowed largely, indeed, of Omar's material, but turning it to a mystical Use more convenient to Themselves and the People they addressed; a People quite as quick of Doubt as of Belief; as keen of Bodily Sense as of Intellectual; and delighting in a cloudy composition of both, in which they could float luxuriously between Heaven and Earth, and this World and the Next, on the wings of a poetical expression, that might serve indifferently for either. Omar was too honest of Heart as well as of Head for this. Having failed (however mistakenly) of finding any Providence but Destiny, and any World but This, he set about making the most of it; preferring rather to soothe the Soul through the Senses into Acquiescence with Things as he saw them, than to perplex it with vain disquietude after what they *might* be. It has been seen, however, that his Worldly Ambition was not exorbitant; and he very likely takes a humorous or perverse pleasure in exalting the gratification of Sense above that of the Intellect, in which he must have taken great delight, although it failed to answer the Questions in which he, in common with all men, was most vitally interested.

For whatever Reason, however, Omar, as before said, has never been popular in his own Country, and therefore has been but scantily transmitted abroad. The MSS. of his Poems, mutilated beyond the average Casualties of Oriental Tran-scription, are so rare in the East as scarce to have reacht Westward at all, in spite of all the acquisitions of Arms and

Science. There is no copy at the India House, none at the Bibliothèque Nationale of Paris. We know but of one in England: No. 140 of the Ouseley MSS. at the Bodleian, written at Shiráz, A.D. 1460. This contains but 158 Rubáiyát. One in the Asiatic Society's Library at Calcutta (of which we have a Copy), contains (and yet incomplete) 516, though swelled to that by all kinds of Repetition and Corruption. So Von Hammer speaks of *his* copy as containing about 200, while Dr. Sprenger catalogues the Lucknow MS. at double that number.* The Scribes, too, of the Oxford and

* "Since this paper was written" (adds the Reviewer in a note), "we have met with a Copy of a very rare Edition, printed at Calcutta in 1836. This contains 438 Tetrastichs, with an Appendix containing 54 others not found in some MSS."

Calcutta MSS. seem to do their Work under a sort of Protest; each beginning with a Tetrastich (whether genuine or not), taken out of its alphabetical order; the Oxford with one of Apology; the Calcutta with one of Expostulation, supposed (says a Notice prefixed to the MS.) to have arisen from a Dream, in which Omar's mother asked about his future fate. It may be rendered thus:—

"Oh Thou who burn'st in Heart for those who burn
In Hell, whose fires thyself shall feed in turn;
How long be crying, 'Mercy on them, God!'
Why, who art Thou to teach, and He to learn?"

The Bodleian Quatrain pleads Pantheism by way of Justification.

"If I myself upon a looser Creed
Have loosely strung the Jewel of Good deed,
Let this one thing for my Atonement plead:
That One for Two I never did mis-read."

The Reviewer,* to whom I owe the Particulars of Omar's Life, concludes his Review by comparing him with Lucretius, both as to natural Temper and Genius, and as acted upon by the Circumstances in which he lived. Both indeed were men of subtle, strong, and cultivated Intellect, fine Imagination, and Hearts passionate for Truth and Justice; who justly revolted from their Country's

* Professor Cowell.

false Religion, and false, or foolish, Devotion to it; but who fell short of replacing what they subverted by such better *Hope* as others, with no better Revelation to guide them, had yet made a Law to themselves. Lucretius, indeed, with such material as Epicurus furnished, satisfied himself with the theory of a vast machine fortuitously constructed, and acting by a Law that implied no Legislator; and so composing himself into a Stoical rather than Epicurean severity of Attitude, sat down to contemplate the mechanical Drama of the Universe which he was part Actor in; himself and all about him (as in his own sublime description of the Roman Theatre) discoloured with the lurid reflex of the Curtain suspended between the

Spectator and the Sun. Omar, more desperate, or more careless of any so complicated System as resulted in nothing but hopeless Necessity, flung his own Genius and Learning with a bitter or humorous jest into the general Ruin which their insufficient glimpses only served to reveal; and, pretending sensual pleasure as the serious purpose of Life, only *diverted* himself with speculative problems of Deity, Destiny, Matter and Spirit, Good and Evil, and other such questions, easier to start than to run down, and the pursuit of which becomes a very weary sport at last!

With regard to the present Translation. The original Rubáiyát (as, missing an Arabic Guttural, these *Tetrastichs* are more musically called) are independent

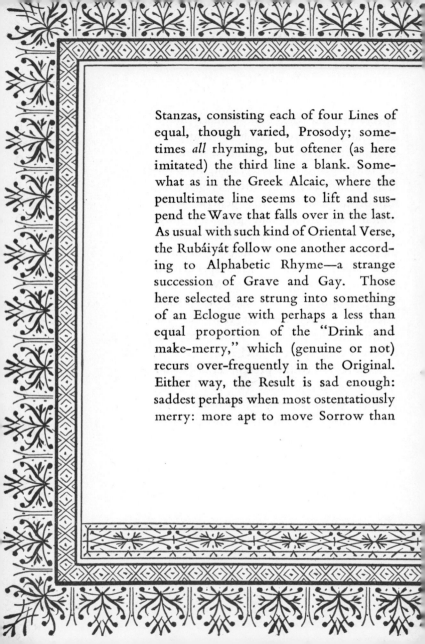

Stanzas, consisting each of four Lines of equal, though varied, Prosody; sometimes *all* rhyming, but oftener (as here imitated) the third line a blank. Somewhat as in the Greek Alcaic, where the penultimate line seems to lift and suspend the Wave that falls over in the last. As usual with such kind of Oriental Verse, the Rubáiyát follow one another according to Alphabetic Rhyme—a strange succession of Grave and Gay. Those here selected are strung into something of an Eclogue with perhaps a less than equal proportion of the "Drink and make-merry," which (genuine or not) recurs over-frequently in the Original. Either way, the Result is sad enough: saddest perhaps when most ostentatiously merry: more apt to move Sorrow than

Anger toward the old Tent-maker, who, after vainly endeavouring to unshackle his Steps from Destiny, and to catch some authentic Glimpse of TO-MORROW, fell back upon TO-DAY (which has outlasted so many To-morrows!) as the only Ground he had got to stand upon, however momentarily slipping from under his Feet.

Edward Fitz Gerald

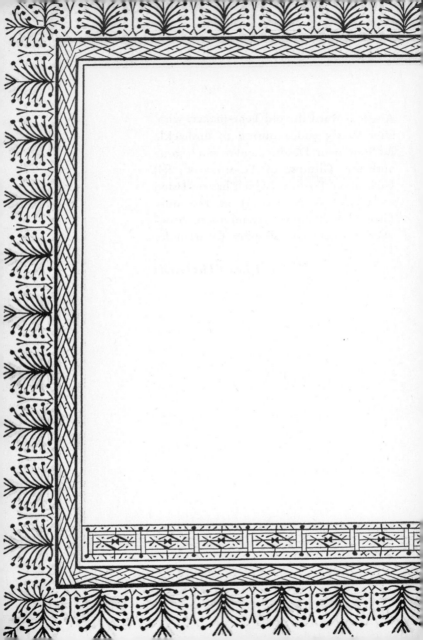

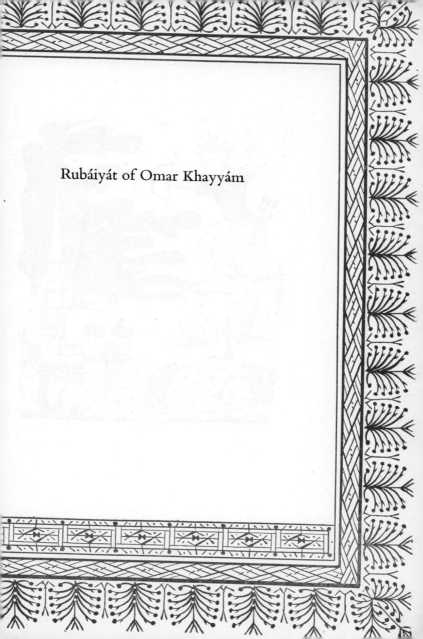

Rubáiyát of Omar Khayyám

I

Wake! For the Sun, who scatter'd into flight
The Stars before him from the Field of Night,
  Drives Night along with them from Heav'n, and strikes
The Sultán's Turret with a Shaft of Light.

II

Before the Phantom of False Morning died,
Methought a Voice within the Tavern cried,
  "When all the Temple is prepared within,
Why nods the drowsy Worshipper outside?"

III

And, as the Cock crew, those who stood before

The Tavern shouted—"Open then the Door!

   You know how little while we have to stay,

And, once departed, may return no more."

IV

Now the New Year reviving old Desires,

The thoughtful Soul to Solitude retires,

   Where the WHITE HAND OF MOSES *on the Boug*

Puts out, and Jesus from the Ground suspires.

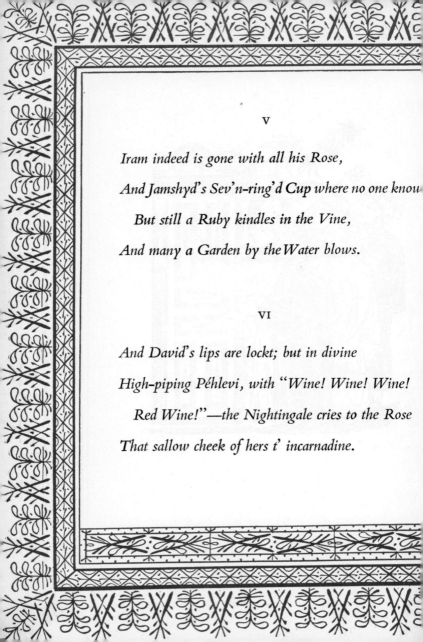

V

Iram indeed is gone with all his Rose,

And Jamshyd's Sev'n-ring'd Cup where no one knou

   But still a Ruby kindles in the Vine,

And many a Garden by the Water blows.

VI

And David's lips are lockt; but in divine

High-piping Péhlevi, with "Wine! Wine! Wine!

   Red Wine!"—the Nightingale cries to the Rose

That sallow cheek of hers t' incarnadine.

VII

Come, fill the Cup, and in the fire of Spring

Your Winter-garment of Repentance fling:

   The Bird of Time has but a little way

To flutter—and the Bird is on the Wing.

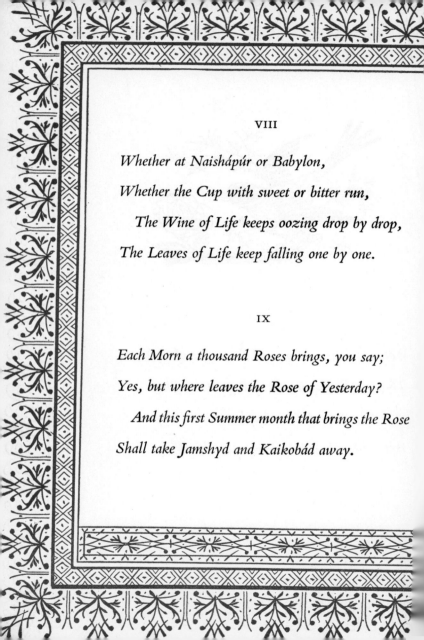

VIII

Whether at Naishápúr or Babylon,

Whether the Cup with sweet or bitter run,

  The Wine of Life keeps oozing drop by drop,

The Leaves of Life keep falling one by one.

IX

Each Morn a thousand Roses brings, you say;

Yes, but where leaves the Rose of Yesterday?

  And this first Summer month that brings the Rose

Shall take Jamshyd and Kaikobád away.

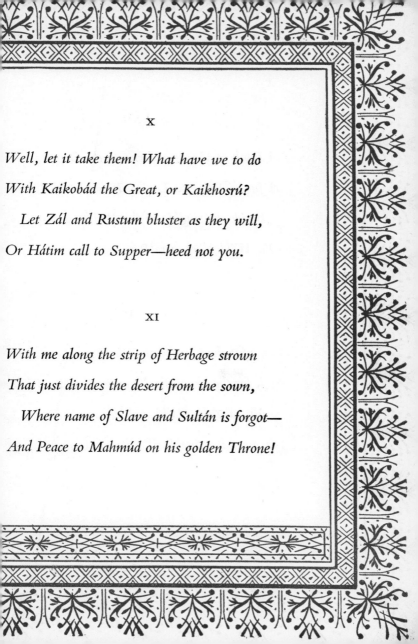

X

Well, let it take them! What have we to do

With Kaikobád the Great, or Kaikhosrú?

   Let Zál and Rustum bluster as they will,

Or Hátim call to Supper—heed not you.

XI

With me along the strip of Herbage strown

That just divides the desert from the sown,

   Where name of Slave and Sultán is forgot—

And Peace to Mahmúd on his golden Throne!

XII

A Book of Verses underneath the Bough,

A Jug of Wine, a Loaf of Bread—and Thou

Beside me singing in the Wilderness—

Oh, Wilderness were Paradise enow!

XIII

Some for the Glories of This World; and some

Sigh for the Prophet's Paradise to come;

Ah, take the Cash, and let the Credit go,

Nor heed the rumble of a distant Drum!

XIV

Look to the blowing Rose about us—"Lo,

Laughing," she says, "into the world I blow,

   At once the silken tassel of my Purse

Tear, and its Treasure on the Garden throw."

XV

And those who husbanded the Golden grain,

And those who flung it to the winds like Rain,

   Alike to no such aureate Earth are turn'd

As, buried once, Men want dug up again.

XVI

The *Worldly* Hope men set their Hearts upon

Turns *Ashes—or it prospers; and anon,*

   Like Snow upon the *Desert's* dusty *Face,*

Lighting a little hour or two—is gone.

XVII

Think, in this batter'd Caravanserai

Whose Portals are alternate Night and Day,

How Sultán after Sultán with his Pomp

Abode his destined Hour, and went his way.

XVIII

They say the Lion and the Lizard keep

The Courts where Jamshyd gloried and drank deep:

And Bahrám, that great Hunter—the Wild Ass

Stamps o'er his Head, but cannot break his Sleep.

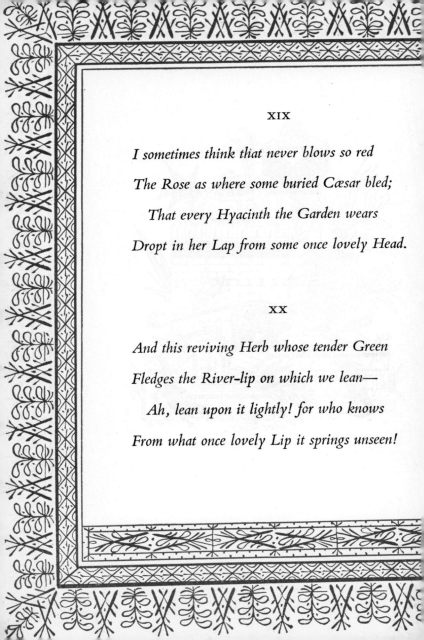

XIX

I sometimes think that never blows so red

The Rose as where some buried Cæsar bled;

That every Hyacinth the Garden wears

Dropt in her Lap from some once lovely Head.

XX

And this reviving Herb whose tender Green

Fledges the River-lip on which we lean—

Ah, lean upon it lightly! for who knows

From what once lovely Lip it springs unseen!

XXI

Ah, my Belovéd, fill the Cup that clears

To-DAY of past Regrets and future Fears:

   To-MORROW!—Why, To-morrow I may be

Myself with Yesterday's Sev'n thousand Years.

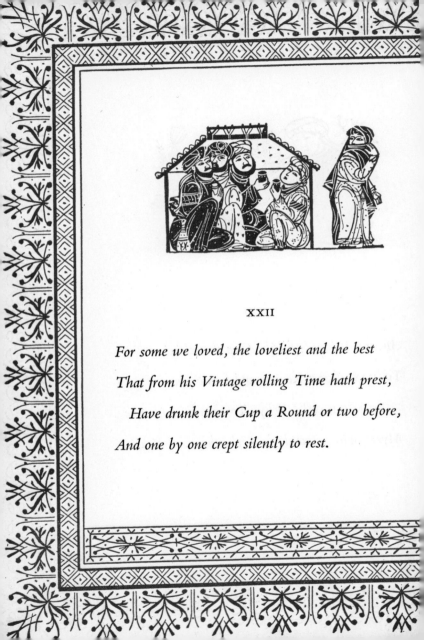

XXII

For some we loved, the loveliest and the best
That from his Vintage rolling Time hath prest,
  Have drunk their Cup a Round or two before,
And one by one crept silently to rest.

XXIII

And we, that now make merry in the Room
They left, and Summer dresses in new bloom,
   Ourselves must we beneath the Couch of Earth
Descend—ourselves to make a Couch—for whom?

XXIV

Ah, make the most of what we yet may spend,
Before we too into the Dust descend;
   Dust into Dust, and under Dust to lie,
Sans Wine, sans Song, sans Singer, and—sans End!

XXV

Alike for those who for To-day prepare,

And those that after some To-morrow stare,

A Muezzín from the Tower of Darkness cries,

"Fools! your Reward is neither Here nor There."

XXVI

Why, all the Saints and Sages who discuss'd

Of the Two Worlds so wisely—they are thrust

   Like foolish Prophets forth; their Words to Scorn

Are scatter'd, and their Mouths are stopt with Dust.

XXVII

Myself when young did eagerly frequent

Doctor and Saint, and heard great argument

   About it and about: but evermore

Came out by the same door where in I went.

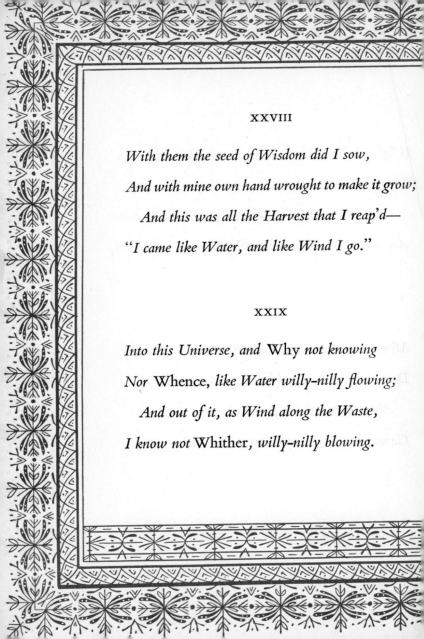

XXVIII

With them the seed of Wisdom did I sow,

And with mine own hand wrought to make it grow;

* And this was all the Harvest that I reap'd—*

"I came like Water, and like Wind I go."

XXIX

Into this Universe, and Why *not knowing*

Nor Whence, *like Water willy-nilly flowing;*

* And out of it, as Wind along the Waste,*

I know not Whither, *willy-nilly blowing.*

XXX

What, without asking, hither hurried Whence?

And, without asking, Whither hurried hence!

   Oh, many a Cup of this forbidden Wine

Must drown the memory of that insolence!

XXXI

Up from Earth's Centre through the Seventh Gate

I rose, and on the Throne of Saturn sate;

   And many a Knot unravel'd by the Road;

But not the Master-knot of Human Fate.

XXXII

There was the Door to which I found no Key;

There was the Veil through which I might not see;

   Some little talk awhile of ME and THEE

There was—and then no more of THEE and ME.

XXXIII

Earth could not answer; nor the Seas that mourn

In flowing Purple, of their Lord forlorn;

   Nor rolling Heaven, with all his Signs reveal'd

And hidden by the sleeve of Night and Morn.

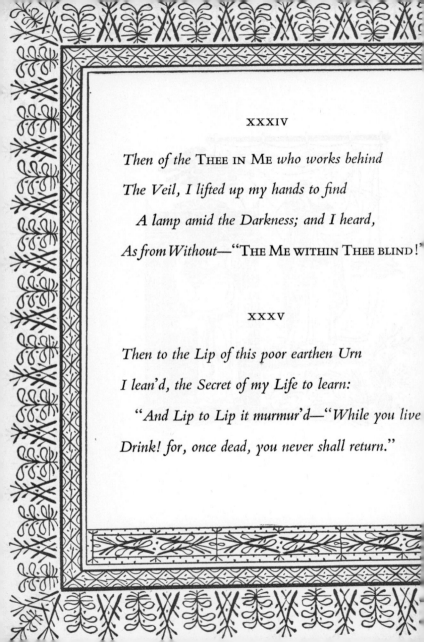

XXXIV

Then of the THEE IN ME who works behind
The Veil, I lifted up my hands to find
  A lamp amid the Darkness; and I heard,
As from Without—"THE ME WITHIN THEE blind!"

XXXV

Then to the Lip of this poor earthen Urn
I lean'd, the Secret of my Life to learn:
  "And Lip to Lip it murmur'd—"While you live
Drink! for, once dead, you never shall return."

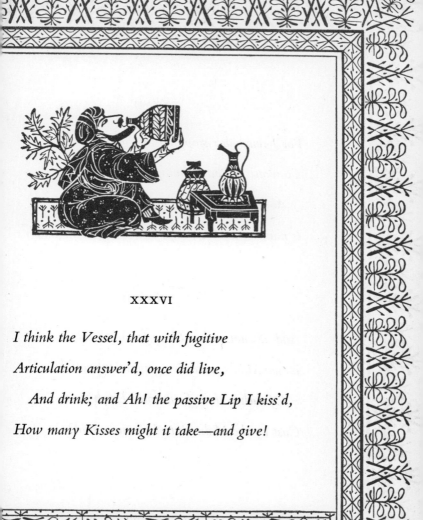

XXXVI

I think the Vessel, that with fugitive

Articulation answer'd, once did live,

And drink; and Ah! the passive Lip I kiss'd,

How many Kisses might it take—and give!

XXXVII

For I remember stopping by the way
To watch a Potter thumping his wet Clay:
And with its all-obliterated Tongue
It murmur'd—"Gently, Brother, gently, pray!"

XXXVIII

And has not such a Story from of Old
Down Man's successive generations roll'd
Of such a clod of saturated Earth
Cast by the Maker into Human mould?

XXXIX

And not a drop that from our Cups we throw

For Earth to drink of, but may steal below

To quench the fire of Anguish in some Eye

There hidden—far beneath, and long ago.

As Then the Tulip for her morning sup

Of Heav'nly Vintage from the soil looks up,

  Do you devoutly do the like, till Heav'n

To Earth invert you—like an empty Cup.

Perplext no more with Human or Divine,

To-morrow's tangle to the winds resign,

  And lose your fingers in the tresses of

The Cypress-slender Minister of Wine.

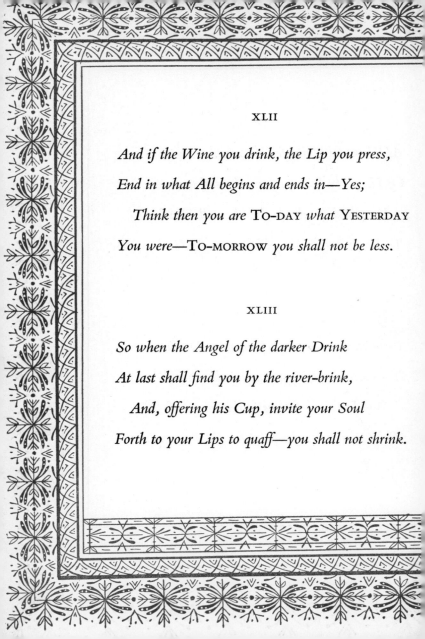

XLII

And if the Wine you drink, the Lip you press,
End in what All begins and ends in—Yes;
  Think then you are TO-DAY what YESTERDAY
You were—TO-MORROW you shall not be less.

XLIII

So when the Angel of the darker Drink
At last shall find you by the river-brink,
  And, offering his Cup, invite your Soul
Forth to your Lips to quaff—you shall not shrink.

XLIV

Why, if the Soul can fling the Dust aside,

And naked on the Air of Heaven ride,

　　Were't not a Shame—were't not a Shame for him

In this clay carcase crippled to abide?

XLV

'Tis but a Tent where takes his one day's rest

A Sultán to the realm of Death addrest;

　　The Sultán rises, and the dark Ferrásh

Strikes, and prepares it for another Guest.

XLVI

And fear not lest Existence closing your

Account, and mine, should know the like no more;

    The Eternal Sákí from that Bowl has pour'd

Millions of Bubbles like us, and will pour.

XLVII

When You and I behind the Veil are past,

Oh, but the long, long while the World shall last,

Which of our Coming and Departure heeds

As the Sea's self should heed a pebble-cast.

XLVIII

A Moment's Halt—a momentary taste

Of Being *from the Well amid the Waste—*

   And Lo!—the phantom Caravan has reach'd

The Nothing *it set out from—Oh, make haste!*

XLIX

Would you that spangle of Existence spend

About the secret—*quick about it, Friend!*

   A Hair perhaps divides the False and True—

And upon what, prithee, may life depend?

67

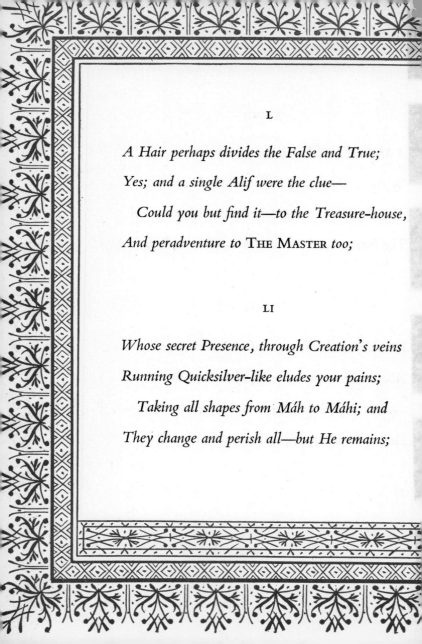

L

A Hair perhaps divides the False and True;

Yes; and a single Alif were the clue—

    Could you but find it—to the Treasure-house,

And peradventure to THE MASTER too;

LI

Whose secret Presence, through Creation's veins

Running Quicksilver-like eludes your pains;

    Taking all shapes from Máh to Máhi; and

They change and perish all—but He remains;

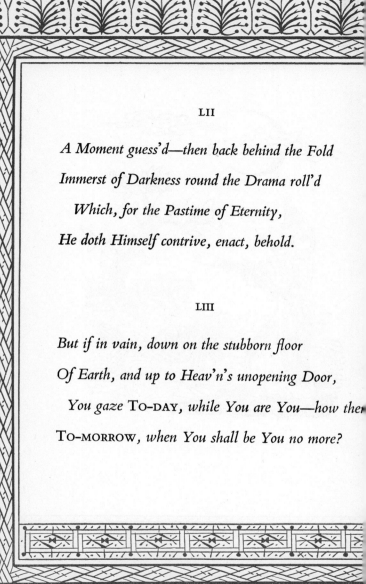

LII

A Moment guess'd—then back behind the Fold
Immerst of Darkness round the Drama roll'd
   Which, for the Pastime of Eternity,
He doth Himself contrive, enact, behold.

LIII

But if in vain, down on the stubborn floor
Of Earth, and up to Heav'n's unopening Door,
   You gaze TO-DAY, while You are You—how then
TO-MORROW, when You shall be You no more?

LIV

Waste not your Hour, nor in the vain pursuit

Of This and That endeavor and dispute;

Better be jocund with the fruitful Grape

Than sadden after none, or bitter, Fruit.

LV

You know, my Friends, with what a brave Carou.

I made a Second Marriage in my house;

   Divorced old barren Reason from my Bed,

And took the Daughter of the Vine to Spouse.

LVI

For "Is" and "Is-not" though with Rule and Li

And "Up-and-down" by Logic I define,

   Of all that one should care to fathom, I

Was never deep in anything but—Wine.

LVII

Ah, but my Computations, People say,

Reduced the Year to better reckoning?—Nay,

'Twas only striking from the Calendar

Unborn To-morrow, and dead Yesterday.

LVIII

And lately, by the Tavern Door agape,

Came shining through the Dusk an Angel Shape

Bearing a Vessel on his Shoulder; and

He bid me taste of it; and 'twas—the Grape!

LIX

The Grape that can with Logic absolute

The Two-and-Seventy jarring Sects confute:

The sovereign Alchemist that in a trice

Life's leaden metal into Gold transmute:

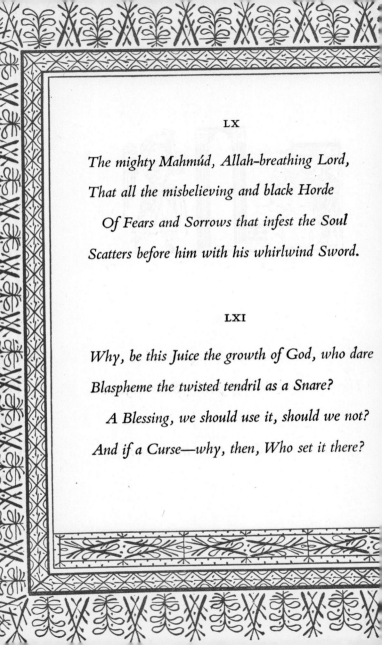

LX

The mighty Mahmúd, Allah-breathing Lord,

That all the misbelieving and black Horde

    Of Fears and Sorrows that infest the Soul

Scatters before him with his whirlwind Sword.

LXI

Why, be this Juice the growth of God, who dare

Blaspheme the twisted tendril as a Snare?

    A Blessing, we should use it, should we not?

And if a Curse—why, then, Who set it there?

LXII

I must adjure the Balm of Life, I must,

Scared by some After-reckoning ta'en on trust,

   Or lured with Hope of some Diviner Drink,

To fill the Cup—when crumbled into Dust!

LXIII

Oh, threats of Hell and Hopes of Paradise!

One thing at least is certain—This Life flies,

   One thing is certain and the rest is Lies;

The Flower that once has blown for ever dies.

LXIV

Strange, is it not? that of the myriads who

Before us pass'd the door of Darkness through,

Not one returns to tell us of the Road,

Which to discover we must travel too.

LXV

The Revelations of Devout and Learn'd
Who rose before us, and as Prophets burn'd,
  Are all but Stories, which awoke from Sleep
They told their comrades, and to Sleep return'd.

LXVI

I sent my Soul through the Invisible,
Some letter of that After-life to spell:
  And by and by my Soul return'd to me,
And answer'd "I Myself am Heav'n and Hell":

LXVII

Heav'n but the Vision of fulfill'd Desire,
And Hell the Shadow from a Soul on fire,
  Cast on the Darkness into which Ourselves,
So late emerged from, shall so soon expire.

LXVIII

We are no other than a moving row
Of Magic Shadow-shapes that come and go
  Round with the Sun-illumined Lantern held
In Midnight by the Master of the Show;

LXIX

But helpless Pieces of the Game He plays

Upon this Chequer-board of Nights and Days;

   Hither and thither moves, and checks, and slays,

And one by one back in the Closet lays.

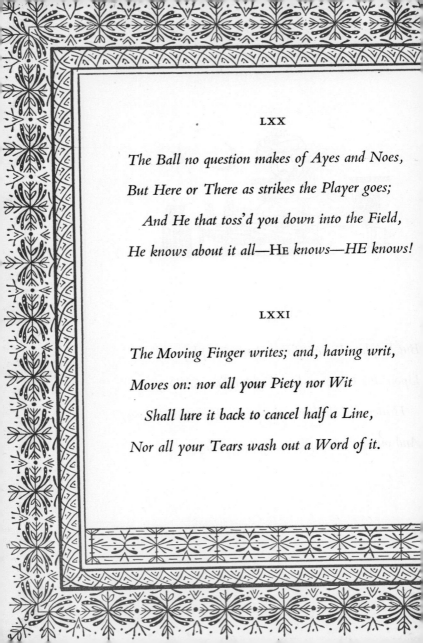

LXX

The Ball no question makes of Ayes and Noes,

But Here or There as strikes the Player goes;

   And He that toss'd you down into the Field,

He knows about it all—HE knows—HE knows!

LXXI

The Moving Finger writes; and, having writ,

Moves on: nor all your Piety nor Wit

   Shall lure it back to cancel half a Line,

Nor all your Tears wash out a Word of it.

LXXII

And that inverted Bowl they call the Sky,

Whereunder crawling coop'd we live and die,

    Lift not your hands to It for help—for It

As impotently moves as you or I.

LXXIII

With Earth's first Clay They did the LastMan knea

And there of the Last Harvest sow'd the Seed:

    And the first Morning of Creation wrote

What the Last Dawn of Reckoning shall read.

LXXIV

esterday This *Day's Madness* did prepare:

O-MORROW'S *Silence, Triumph, or Despair:*

Drink! for you know not whence you came, nor why:

rink! *for you know not why you go, nor where.*

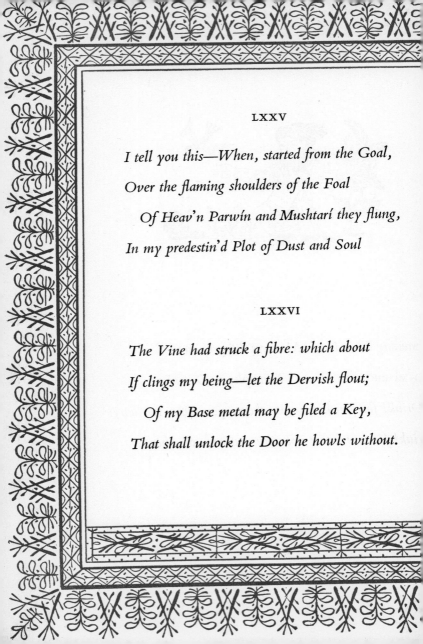

LXXV

I tell you this—When, started from the Goal,

Over the flaming shoulders of the Foal

   Of Heav'n Parwín and Mushtarí they flung,

In my predestin'd Plot of Dust and Soul

LXXVI

The Vine had struck a fibre: which about

If clings my being—let the Dervish flout;

   Of my Base metal may be filed a Key,

That shall unlock the Door he howls without.

LXXVII

And this I know: whether the one True Light

Kindle to Love, or Wrath-consume me quite,

  One Flash of It within the Tavern caught

Better than in the Temple lost outright.

LXXVIII

What! out of senseless Nothing to provoke

A conscious Something to resent the yoke

  Of unpermitted Pleasure, under pain

Of Everlasting Penalties, if broke!

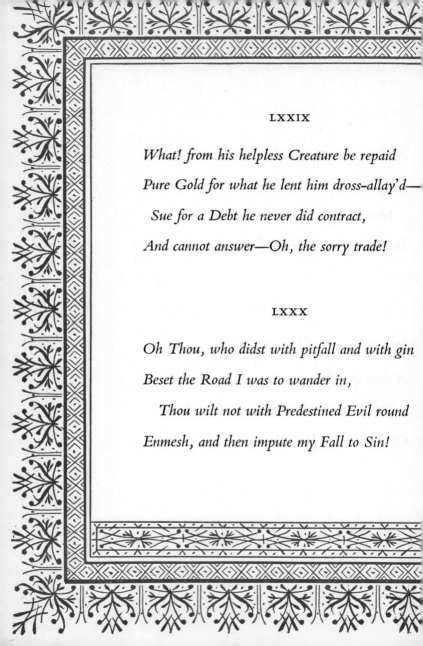

LXXIX

What! from his helpless Creature be repaid
Pure Gold for what he lent him dross-allay'd—
  Sue for a Debt he never did contract,
And cannot answer—Oh, the sorry trade!

LXXX

Oh Thou, who didst with pitfall and with gin
Beset the Road I was to wander in,
  Thou wilt not with Predestined Evil round
Enmesh, and then impute my Fall to Sin!

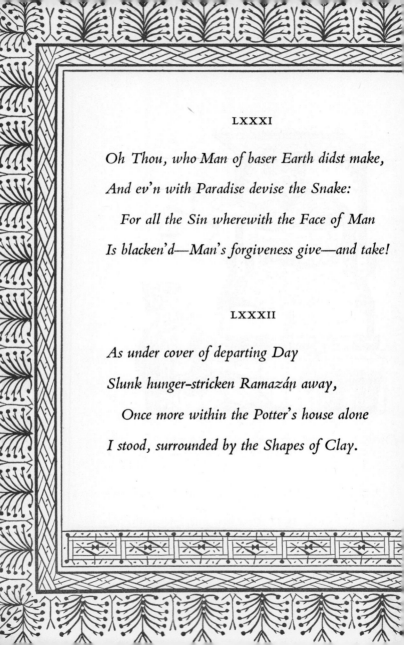

LXXXI

Oh Thou, who Man of baser Earth didst make,
And ev'n with Paradise devise the Snake:
  For all the Sin wherewith the Face of Man
Is blacken'd—Man's forgiveness give—and take!

LXXXII

As under cover of departing Day
Slunk hunger-stricken Ramazán away,
  Once more within the Potter's house alone
I stood, surrounded by the Shapes of Clay.

LXXXIII

Shapes of all Sorts and Sizes, great and small,

That stood along the floor and by the wall;

* And some loquacious Vessels were; and some*

Listen'd perhaps, but never talk'd at all.

LXXXIV

Said one among them—"Surely not in vain
My substance of the common Earth was ta'en
   And to this Figure moulded, to be broke,
Or trampled back to shapeless Earth again."

LXXXV

Then said a Second—"Ne'er a peevish Boy
Would break the Bowl from which he drank in joy;
   And He that with His hand the Vessel made
Will surely not in after Wrath destroy."

LXXXVI

After a momentary silence spake
Some Vessel of a more ungainly Make:
  "They sneer at me for leaning all awry:
What! did the Hand then of the Potter shake?"

LXXXVII

Whereat some one of the loquacious Lot—
I think a Súfi pipkin—waxing hot—
  "All this of Pot and Potter—Tell me then,
Who is the Potter, pray, and who the Pot?"

LXXXVIII

"Why," said another, "Some there are who tell
Of one who threatens he will toss to Hell
    The luckless Pots he marr'd in making—Pish!
He's a Good Fellow, and 'twill all be well."

LXXXIX

"Well," murmur'd one, "Let whoso make or buy,
My Clay with long Oblivion is gone dry:
    But fill me with the old familiar Juice,
Methinks I might recover by and by."

XC

So while the Vessels one by one were speaking,

The little Moon look'd in that all were seeking:

   And then they jogg'd each other, "Brother! Brother!

Now for the Porter's shoulder-knot a-creaking!"

XCI

Ah, with the Grape my fading Life provide,

And wash the Body whence the Life has died,

   And lay me, shrouded in the living Leaf,

By some not unfrequented Garden-side.

XCII

That ev'n my buried Ashes such a snare

Of Vintage shall fling up into the Air

   As not a True-believer passing by

But shall be overtaken unaware.

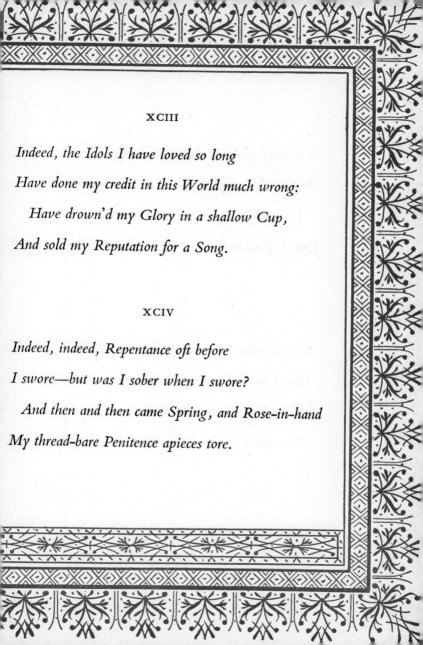

XCIII

Indeed, the Idols I have loved so long

Have done my credit in this World much wrong:

   Have drown'd my Glory in a shallow Cup,

And sold my Reputation for a Song.

XCIV

Indeed, indeed, Repentance oft before

I swore—but was I sober when I swore?

   And then and then came Spring, and Rose-in-hand

My thread-bare Penitence apieces tore.

XCV

And much as Wine has play'd the Infidel,

And robb'd me of my Robe of Honour—Well,

I wonder often what the Vintners buy

One half so precious as the stuff they sell.

XCVI

Yet Ah, that Spring should vanish with the Rose!

That Youth's sweet-scented manuscript should close!

The Nightingale that in the branches sang,

Ah, whence, and whither flown again, who knows!

XCVII

Would but the Desert of the Fountain yield

One glimpse—if dimly, yet indeed, reveal'd,

* To which the fainting Traveller might spring,*

As springs the trampled herbage of the field!

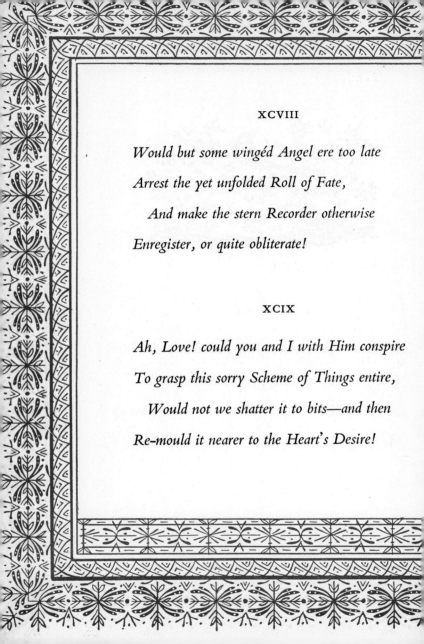

XCVIII

Would but some wingéd Angel ere too late

Arrest the yet unfolded Roll of Fate,

    And make the stern Recorder otherwise

Enregister, or quite obliterate!

XCIX

Ah, Love! could you and I with Him conspire

To grasp this sorry Scheme of Things entire,

    Would not we shatter it to bits—and then

Re-mould it nearer to the Heart's Desire!

C

Yon rising Moon that looks for us again—
How oft hereafter will she wax and wane;
*   How oft hereafter rising look for us*
Through this same Garden—and for one in vain!

CI

And when like her, oh Sákí, you shall pass
Among the Guests Star-scatter'd on the Grass,
*   And in your joyous errand reach the spot*
Where I made One—turn down an empty Glass!

TAMÁM